Come To Prayer

Salwah Isaacs-Johaadien   Illustrated by Zeynep Yildirim

A blanket of snow, icy and thick,
Has covered the city of Reykjavik.

Warm, woolly blankets come off with a kick,
We'll go out for Fajr; no, we won't get sick.

Come to **prayer.**

Come to **Salah.**

Hours of rain are set to continue,
Drenching the city of Honolulu.

6

I don't think we'll need the dugout canoe,
A slow drive to Zuhr; that's what we will do.

Come to **success**.

Come to **falah**.

The beaches are fine and the breeze is mellow,
It feels like a holiday here in Rio.

Quickly eat up your brigadeiro.
Let's pray Asr before the sun turns yellow.

Come to **prayer.**

Come to **salah.**

12

A mighty sandstorm is sweeping through,
Across the Sahara brushing Timbuktu.

14

Our turbans are wrapped, with eyes peering through.
We'll gather for Maghrib, even if we are few.

Come to **success.**

Come to **falah.**

Thunder and lightning have halted our tour.
It's risky to be out in Kuala Lumpur.

18

Let's wait at the masjid where it is secure.
We'll get to pray Isha together for sure.

Come to prayer.

Come to Salah.

Come to Success.

Come to falah.

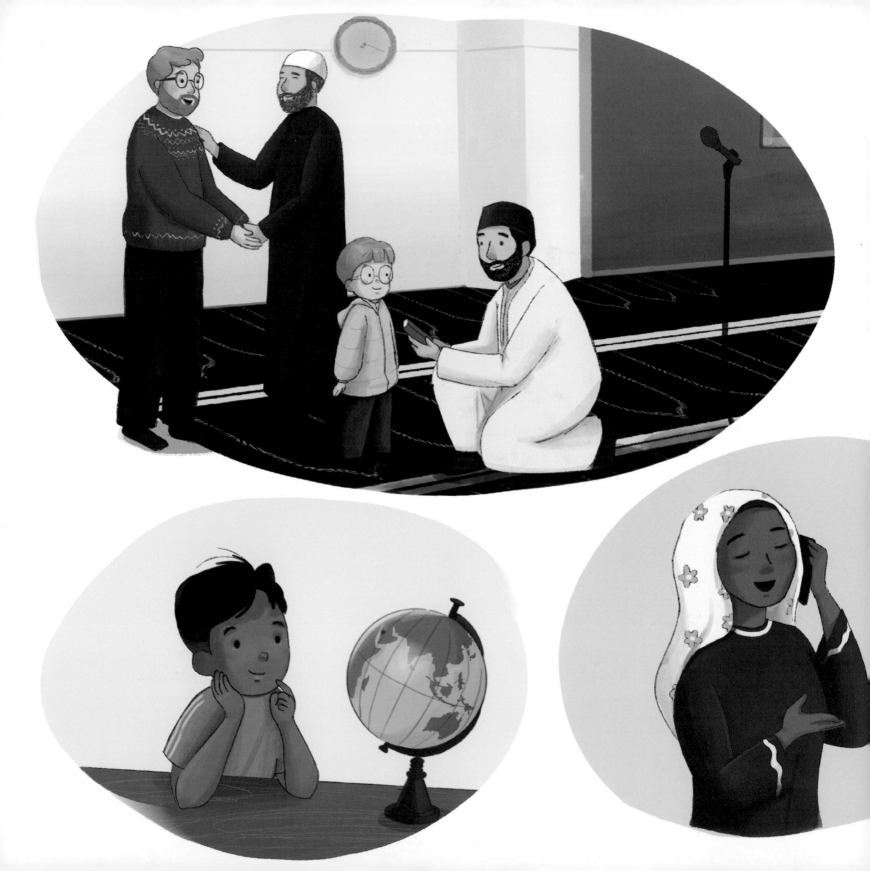

The air is warm and the morning is calm.
We've come from afar, united by Islam.

We enter into Makkah wearing ihraam.
Praying side-by-side in Masjid al-Haram.

Come to **prayer.**

Come to **Salah.**

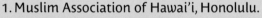

1. Muslim Association of Hawai'i, Honolulu.
2. The Islamic Centre of America, North America.
3. The Grand Mosque of Iceland, Iceland.
4. Al Fozan Mosque, Brussels.
5. Koutoubia Mosque, Morocco.
6. Djinguereber Mosque, Mali.
7. Mesquita da Luz, Brazil.
8. Qolsharif Mosque, Russia.
9. Suleymaniye Mosque, Turkey.
10. Al-Aqsa Mosque and Dome of the Rock, Jerusalem.
11. Masjid al Nabawi, Madinah.
12. Masjid al Haram, Makkah.
13. Mashkhur Jusup Central Mosque, Kazakhstan.
14. Shah Faisal Mosque, Pakistan.
15. Great Mosque of Xi'an, China.
16. Federal Territory Mosque, Malaysia.
17. Grand Mosque of West Sumatra, Indonesia.
18. Sunshine Mosque, Australia.

8

Come to **success.**

13

9

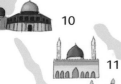
10

14

11

15

12

16

Come to **falah.**

17

18

Come to Prayer

First Published in 2023 by
THE ISLAMIC FOUNDATION

Distributed by
KUBE PUBLISHING LTD
Tel +44 (0)1530 249230, Fax +44 (0)1530 249656
E-mail: info@kubepublishing.com
Website: www.kubepublishing.com

Author Salwah Isaacs-Johaadien
Illustrator Zeynep Yildirim
Book design Nasir Cadir

A Cataloguing-in-Publication Data record for this book is available
from the British Library

ISBN 978-0-86037-901-0
eISBN 978-0-86037-906-5

Printed in China